The Music Did It

Fulton Books
Meadville, PA

Published by Fulton Books 2023

ISBN 979-8-88982-521-0 (paperback)
ISBN 979-8-88982-522-7 (digital)

Printed in the United States of America

The Music Did It

Cheryl Duke

Gabrielle was in a pickle; he was not quite sure what to do now. The Lord told him to call Lucifer for advice. Lucifer could not handle his ten thousand Black people either.

Lucifer said they put out his fire and tried to install air-conditioning.

Since the moment they arrived in this holy place, they had done everything their way no matter the rules that everyone else abided by.

They listened to a different drummer, so to speak. How they ever made it to heaven was between them and their Maker.

There had been a problem with the halos—something to do about hair. Then there were the barbecue stains on the choir robes. Gabrielle shook his head; how was he to keep up with these complaints? He had to find a way to smooth out the way.

Gabrielle had heard there had been trouble that morning at the newcomers' picnic. They had gathered together to bless the event with song, and that's when all the trouble started.

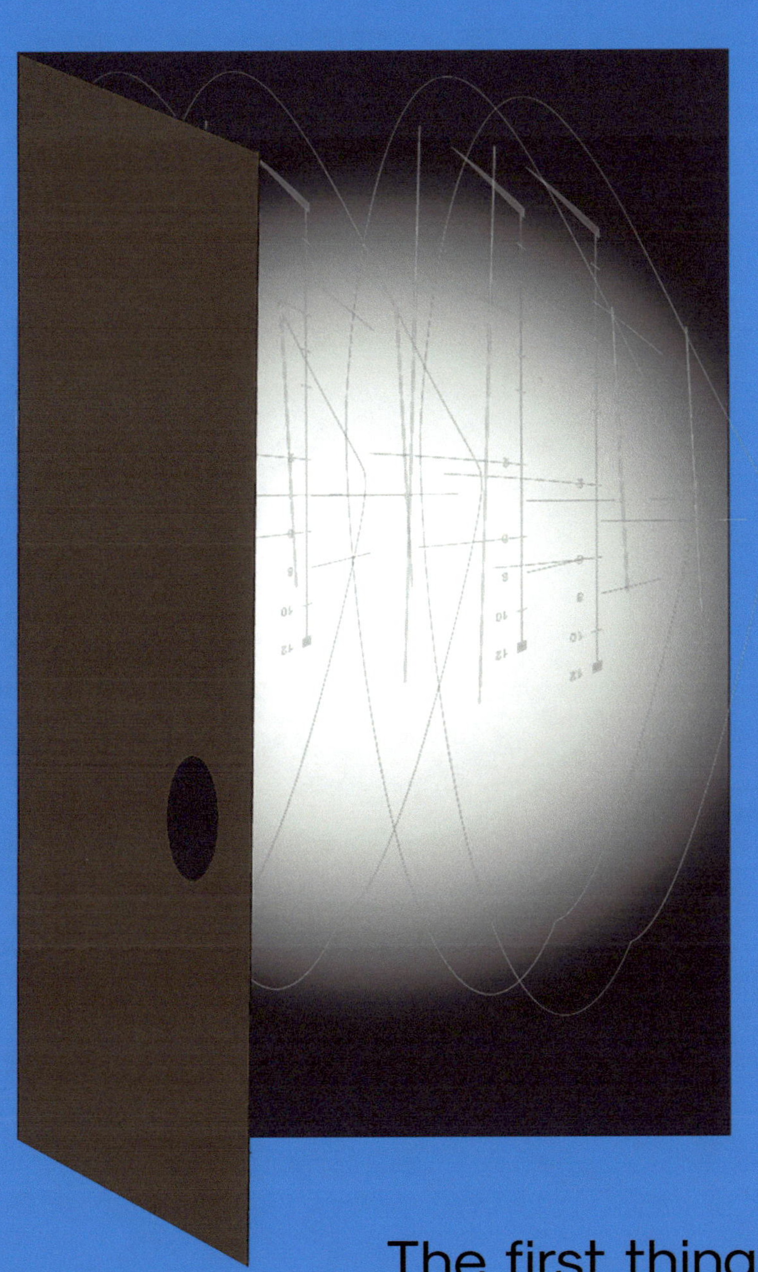

The first thing he would do was talk to
the Lord. Then he would act.

The two young souls that started all the trouble were to put together a praise song incorporating rap, hip-hop, rhythm and blues and, to spice things up, some jazz.

They had a week to work on their praise music. Gabrielle hoped that they would learn to get along as well as create some wonderful music to please God. Talent alone would not be enough.

Those ten thousand Black souls were so excited. All they could talk about was singing before the throne of the Most High. Everyone wanted a chance to sing before the throne of God.

Oh, you should have seen how they acted on audition day. They all lined up, the ones who wanted to sing. The smallest to the biggest were in that line.

The first day of choir rehearsal was chaotic. Everyone wanted to sing a solo. When they did sing, it was not together, not as a choir. They sang off-key, and they sang out of tune, and they sang too loud, and they sang too low.

By the end of the first week, they were coming together. Only a
few needed extra care. Gabrielle was ecstatic.

All of heaven gave a joyful noise unto the Lord as the choir sang in praise and worship a new song.

About the Author

Cheryl Duke has been a storyteller all her life. Even as a child, she was compelled to make up and recite stories to anyone who dared to listen. Around a campfire or on a road trip, it was her pleasure to entertain her captive audience. As a young woman, Cheryl joined the Black Storytellers Alliance in Minneapolis. She delighted the young as well as the old with her ancient stories and ones she created on the spot. It is not until recently that she had the courage to write them down.